12 Christmas Favorites

Low Voice

Edited by Richard Walters

Caroling, Caroling · The Christmas Song · Do You Hear What I Hear ·
Gesù Bambino · Go, Tell It on the Mountain · I Heard the Bells on Christmas Day ·
I Wonder as I Wander · I'll Be Home for Christmas · O Holy Night · Silver Bells ·
Some Children See Him · White Christmas

ISBN 978-0-634-08218-4

CORPORATION
7777 W. BLUEMOUND RD. P.O. BOX 13819 MILWAUKEE, WI 53213

Visit Hal Leonard Online at
www.halleonard.com

Contents

Singers on the CD:
*Kathleen Sonnentag, mezzo-soprano; **Kurt Ollmann, baritone

Pianist on the CD:
Richard Walters

Violinist on the CD:
Christopher Ruck (tracks 4, 16)

Caroling, Caroling

Words by Wihla Hutson
Music by Alfred Burt

sweet and clear, Sing the sad of heart to cheer.
song we sing, Glad - some tid - ings now we bring.
hap - py morn, "Lo, the King of heav'n is born."

1,2
Ding, dong, ding, dong, Christ - mas bells are ring - ing.

3
Ding, dong, ding, dong,

Ding, dong, ding, dong, Christ - mas bells are ring - ing.

Do You Hear What I Hear

Words and Music by Noel Regney
and Gloria Shayne

where, Lis - ten to what I say! _____ The

Child; The Child, sleep-ing in the night; He will bring us good - ness and

opt.

light, He will bring us good - ness and

light. _____

The Christmas Song
(Chestnuts Roasting on an Open Fire)

Music and Lyric by Mel Torme
and Robert Wells
Arranged by Richard Walters

help to make the sea - son bright. Ti - ny tots with their

eyes all a - glow will find it hard to sleep to - night. They __ know that

San - ta's __ on his way; he's __ load - ed lots of toys __ and good - ies __ on his

sleigh, and __ ev - 'ry moth - er's child _____ is __ gon - na spy to __ see if

Gesù Bambino
(with optional violin or cello obbligato)

Text by Frederick H. Martens
Music by Pietro A. Yon

* Omit small notes when performing this song with violin or cello.

an - gels sang, _ the shep-herds sang, The grate - ful earth re - joiced, _____ And at __ His bless - ed

birth the stars Their ex - ul - ta - tion voiced. _____ O come let us a -
opt: Ve - ni - te a - do -

Non troppo lento

dore Him, __ O come let us a - dore Him, _____ O
re - mus, Ve - ni - te a - do - re - mus, _____ Ve-

Violin
Gesù Bambino

Text by Frederick H. Martens
Music by Pietro A. Yon

This part may be carefully cut from the book.

continued on page 21

Cello
Gesù Bambino

Text by Frederick H. Martens
Music by Pietro A. Yon

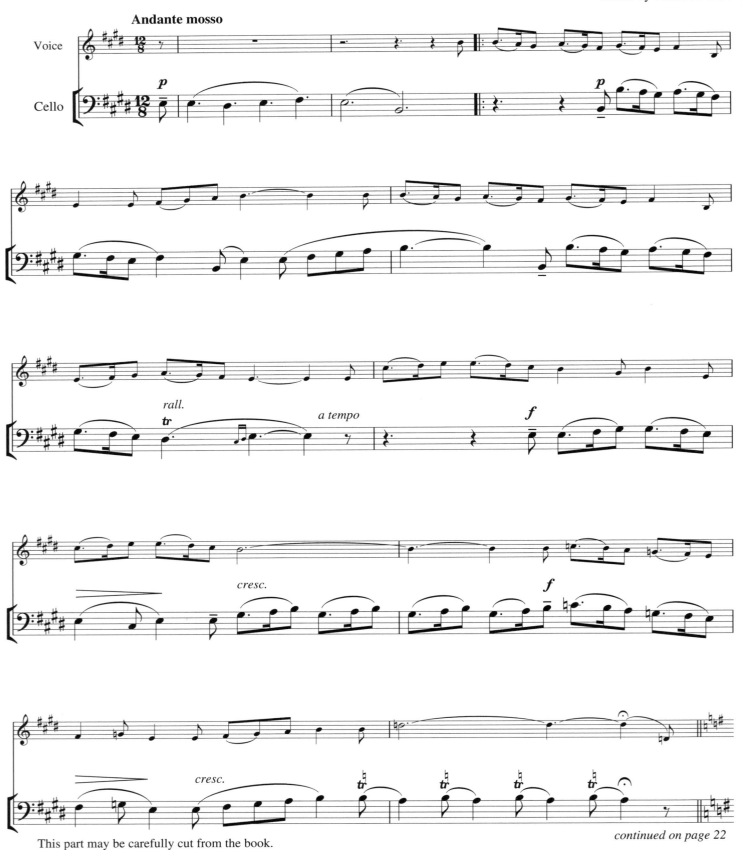

This part may be carefully cut from the book.

continued on page 22

Violin

Cello

I Heard the Bells on Christmas Day

Music by Johnny Marks
Words by Henry Wadsworth Longfellow
Adapted by Johnny Marks
Arranged by Luke Duane

peace on earth good will to men.

And in de - spair, I

bowed my head, "There is no peace on earth," I said. "For hate is strong and

mocks the song of peace on earth, good will to men." Then

Go, Tell It on the Mountain

African-American Spiritual
Arranged by Harry T. Burleigh
Verses by John W. Work, Jr.

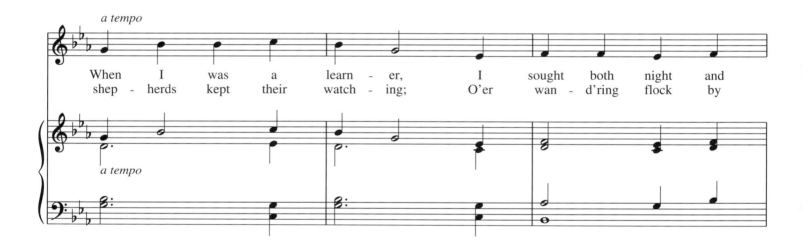

Burleigh's arrangement was originally titled "Go Tell It on De Mountains." The singular form "mountain" has become the standard version for this song.

He show me the way. ___ Go tell it on the
shone a ho - ly light. ___

moun - tain; O - ver the hills an' ev - 'ry - where:

Go tell it on the moun - tain, Our Je - sus Christ __ is

born.

* On the companion recording we have eliminated this repeat (and the 3rd verse), because this setting may feel too long for some situations.

I Wonder as I Wander
(Appalachian Carol)

Collected, adapted, and arranged by John Jacob Niles

When Ma - ry birthed Je - sus, 'twas in a cow's stall, With

wise men and farm - ers and shep - herds and all. But high from God's heav - en a

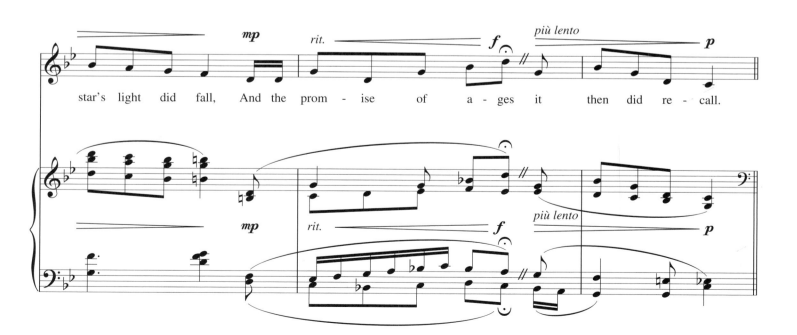

star's light did fall, And the prom - ise of a - ges it then did re - call.

I won-der as I wan-der, out un-der the sky, How Je-sus the Sav-ior did come for to die For poor on-'ry peo-ple like

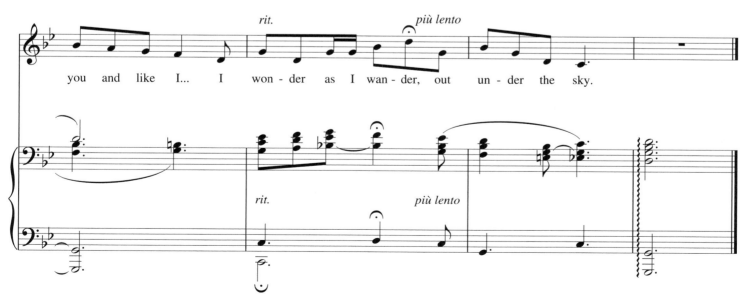

you and like I... I won-der as I wan-der, out un-der the sky.

I'll Be Home for Christmas

Words and Music by Kim Gannon
and Walter Kent
Arranged by Luke Duane

Moderately slow

I'll be home for Christ - mas, _____ you can count on me. _____

Please have snow and mis - tle - toe and pres - ents on the tree. _____

Eve will find me _____ where the love - light gleams. _____ I'll be home for Christ - mas, _____ if on - ly in my dreams. _____

Silver Bells
from the Paramount Picture THE LEMON DROP KID

Words and Music by Jay Livingston
and Ray Evans
Arranged by Luke Duane

here is what Christ - mas time means to

8va (both hands)

rit.

Entrance

Easily

me.

Cit - y side - walks, bus - y side - walks dressed in
street lights, e - ven stop - lights blink a

rit.

mp

hol - i - day style; In the air there's a feel - ing of
bright red and green as the shop - pers rush home with their

Christ - mas. _____ Chil - dren laugh - ing, peo - ple pass - ing, meet - ing
treas - ures. _____ Hear the snow crunch, see the kids bunch, this is

hear them ring, _____ soon it will

be Christ - mas Day. _____

Strings of be Christ - mas Day. _____

8va (both hands)

8va

rit.

8va

p

Some Children See Him

Lyric by Wihla Hutson
Music by Alfred Burt

1. Some chil-dren see Him lil-y white, The
   chil-dren see Him al-mond eyed, This
   chil-dren in each dif-f'rent place Will

Ba-by Je-sus born this night. Some chil-dren see Him lil-y white, With
Sav-iour whom we kneel be-side, Some chil-dren see Him al-mond eyed, With
see the Ba-by Je-sus' face Like theirs, but bright with heav'n-ly grace, And

White Christmas
from the Motion Picture Irving Berlin's HOLIDAY INN

Words and Music by
Irving Berlin
Arranged by Richard Walters

Lyrics:

The sun is shin - ing, the grass is green, — The or - ange and palm trees sway; There's nev - er been such a day in Bev - er - ly Hills L. A. But it's De - cem - ber the twen - ty fourth,

and I am long - ing to be up north.

Espressivo

I'm dream - ing of a white

Christ - mas just like the ones I used to know

where the tree tops glis - ten and chil - dren

listen to hear sleigh bells in the snow.

I'm dream-ing of a white

Christ-mas. With ev-'ry Christ-mas card I write:

"May your days be mer-ry___ and bright,

and may all your Christ - mas - es be

white."

Where the tree tops glis - ten and

chil - dren lis - ten to hear

opt.

sleigh bells in the snow.

(poco rit.)

mp

I'm dream - ing of a white Christ - mas;

mf

with ev - 'ry Christ - mas card I write:

mf

O Holy Night
(Cantique de Noël)

French Words by Placide Cappeau
English Words by John S. Dwight
Music by Adolphe Adam

O ho - ly night! The stars are bright - ly shin - ing, It is the night of our dear Sav - iour's birth; Long lay the world in sin and er - ror

Mi - nuit, Chré - tien, c'est l'heu - re so - len - nel - le Où l'Hom - me - Dieu des - cen - dit jus - qu'a nous, Pour ef - fa - cer la ta - che o - ri - gi -

vine! _____ O night, O _____ night di -
ël! _____ voi - ci le _____ Ré - demp-

dim.

vine.
teur.

mf

Tru - ly He taught us to love one an -
Le Ré - demp - teur a bri - sé toute en -

oth - er; His law is love and His Gos - pel is Peace.
tra - ve, La terre est li - bre et le ciel est ou - vert.

Chains shall He break, for the slave is our
Il voit un frè - re_où né - tait qu'un es-

broth - er, And in His name____ all op - pres - sion shall
cla - ve, L'a-mour u - nit____ ceux qu'en-chaî - nait le

cease. Sweet hymns of joy in
fer. Qui lui di - ra no -

grate - ful cho - rus raise we, Let all with - in us
tre re - con - nais-san - ce? C'est pour nous tous qu'il